C000144917

PETER DOYLE

FIRST WORLD WAR
LEADERS AND
COMMANDERS

First published 2014

The History Press
The Mill, Brimscombe Port
Stroud, Gloucestershire, GL5 2QG
www.thehistorypress.co.uk

© Peter Doyle, 2014

The right of Peter Doyle to be identified as the Author
of this work has been asserted in accordance with the
Copyright, Designs and Patents Act 1988.

All rights reserved. No part of this book may be reprinted
or reproduced or utilised in any form or by any electronic,
mechanical or other means, now known or hereafter invented,
including photocopying and recording, or in any information
storage or retrieval system, without the permission in writing
from the Publishers.

British Library Cataloguing in Publication Data.
A catalogue record for this book is available from the British Library.

ISBN 978 0 7509 5570 6

Typesetting and origination by The History Press
Printed in Europe

CONTENTS

INTRODUCTION

TENSIONS IN EUROPE since the Franco-Prussian War of 1870–71 – and the ascension of a new Kaiser, Wilhelm II, to the throne of the German Empire in 1888 – led to power shifts. This meant the development of a new understanding between France and Britain, who put aside their imperial differences in the signing of the Entente Cordiale in 1904. This agreement was followed by the Triple Entente of France, Britain and Russia in 1907. Though not a formal alliance, the Triple Entente nevertheless brought three European nations together in a defensive understanding that gave some protection in the face of attack, with the focus on the Central Powers of Germany and Austria-Hungary, situated at the heart of Europe. Between them, in the west, was the neutral state of Belgium, its borders guaranteed by all the main European signatories, including Britain, Germany and France.

The German Empire was created from a federation of states united by its first chancellor, Otto von Bismarck, in the wake of the victory over France in the Franco-Prussian War of 1870–71. The Dual Alliance, in October 1879, locked Germany and Austria-Hungary together with the guarantee of military aid in the case of attack by Russia. It also promised 'benevolent neutrality' should 'another European country' –

namely France – attack either of their nations. The Ottomans, defeated by Russia in 1878, were also to be courted.

The declaration of war between Austria-Hungary and Serbia in 1914 initiated world conflict; with Germany and Russia supporting their allies, the stage was set, and one by one nations were brought into the fray: France and Britain, Ottoman Turkey and Italy, and ultimately the United States in 1917. There were many other contributions from other nations, Serbia, Japan, Bulgaria, Portugal and Romania among them. This *5 Minute History* focuses on the principal nations and their leaders, and the military commanders who led their armies in battle. It focuses on the main personalities, the generals that shaped the battles or suffered the defeats. A book of this size can never hope to be comprehensive, with some smaller nations omitted, but the main participants, their words and deeds, are here.

PART 1

THE ENTENTE POWERS

GREAT BRITAIN

GREAT BRITAIN, ONE of the three main Entente Powers, came into the war following the invasion of Belgium on 4 August 1914.

THE LEADERS

Herbert Asquith

Herbert Asquith was prime minister when Britain went to war in 1914. A liberal politician, he was well known as an orator, and had been in the post since 1908. With David Lloyd George as his Chancellor of the Exchequer, he selected Kitchener as his Secretary of State for War. In May 1915, Asquith formed a Coalition government in order to create a more solid basis for a wartime administration. But 1915 was a difficult year, especially when the British offensives at Neuve Chappelle, Aubers Ridge and Festubert were fought without satisfactory artillery preparation and with an inadequate supply of shells. With the newspaper giant

---

DID YOU KNOW?

Raymond Asquith, the prime minister's son, served with the Grenadier Guards as a lieutenant and was mortally wounded on the Somme while leading his men into action, on 15 September 1915.

Lord Northcliffe leading the assault against the prime minister, the Conservatives in the Coalition started to question his ability. Though the 'Shell Scandal', as it was known, was solved by forming the Ministry of Munitions to co-ordinate supply and step up manufacturing, it was the increasing number of casualties that made things intolerable for the prime minister, particularly in the wake of the Battle of the Somme. But it was Lloyd George who would signal the end of Asquith's time in office. Manoeuvring behind the scenes, Lloyd George proposed a War Committee that could handle the day-to-day conduct of the conflict. Under pressure from the press, Asquith finally resigned on 5 December 1916; Lloyd George stepped into his place to lead a new Coalition the next day.

David Lloyd George

Lloyd George is known as one of the most charismatic politicians of his age; a lawyer by profession, he became a Liberal MP in North Wales, and with his penchant for oratory was soon in the public eye, rising through the political ranks to serve as Chancellor of the Exchequer. In this post, Lloyd George introduced social reforms that included improvements to social care and the introduction of National Insurance and pensions for old people.

DID YOU KNOW?

Lloyd George was committed to the raising of an entire army corps of Welsh soldiers – men who would serve together and who would wear a uniform of homespun Welsh cloth. This dream did not come to fruition, though the 38th (Welsh) Division served with distinction.

On the eve of war, Lloyd George and three other senior figures expressed their opposition to the coming conflict; whilst the others resigned, the Welshman was persuaded to stay, and served with distinction in the wartime government.

The Shell Scandal of 1915, when British guns were left without sufficient ammunition, rocked the government. Lloyd George was put in place to lead the Ministry of Munitions, which would ensure that shortages would eventually become a thing of the past. From opposing the war to ensuring its successful conclusion, Lloyd George was tireless – and considering the conduct of the war was beyond one man, he schemed for a War Committee to run the conflict. This plan was successful, at the cost of Asquith's resignation; in his place came the Welshman, who formed a new Coalition government in 1916.

I WAS THERE

Once he had taken up war as his metier he seemed to breathe its true spirit; all other thoughts and schemes were abandoned, and he lived for, thought of and talked of nothing but the war.

Max Aitken, talking of Lloyd George, 1928[1]

DID YOU KNOW?

Still committed to social reforms, Lloyd George promised he would create a 'land fit for heroes' for the returning soldiers; with opposition in his Coalition government, he could not deliver on his word.

The new prime minister and the commander-in-chief, Sir Douglas Haig, did not see eye to eye, especially as he tired of the deadlocked trench warfare battles on the Western Front, and sought to divert resources elsewhere, to battlefronts considered to be 'sideshows' by many of the generals. Despite this difference of opinion, Lloyd George stuck with Haig, as there were few others that could step into the breach. At the end of the war, Lloyd George was pressed for a fair settlement with Germany at Versailles, fearing the defeated nation would be plunged into revolution.

Field Marshal Herbert Kitchener

When Field Marshal Earl Kitchener of Khartoum took over as Secretary of State for War in August 1914, he was Britain's most famous soldier, having served with distinction in the Sudan and in the Boer War. With war declared, Asquith turned to Kitchener to be his Secretary of State – though this was not without risk, as, typically of many military men, he had a distrust of politicians. Known to be strong-minded and autocratic, Kitchener was also aware that in all likelihood the war would be long, and, faced with a limited but professional army, he was quick to understand that it would be costly in manpower. Kitchener made a direct appeal to the public, not being confident that the Territorial battalions could be sufficiently flexible to allow rapid expansion, and he set his sights on expanding the army by 500,000 men, with separate appeals, in 100,000 tranches. The Shell Scandal of 1915 hurt Kitchener's reputation, particularly as the Ministry of War was also responsible for the supply chain of munitions. Gallipoli, too, was damaging – even though Kitchener was never fully committed to it – and His reputation was in decline. Nevertheless, when the Tsar requested Kitchener visit Russia in 1916 to help bolster national support for the war, he agreed to go. This was a fatal mistake:

DID YOU KNOW?

Arguably the most famous poster ever produced depicts Lord Kitchener's staring eyes and pointing finger, intended to induce passers-by to 'Join their Country's Army'. There are many versions.

I WAS THERE

Lord Kitchener now came forward to the Cabinet, on almost the first occasion after he joined us, and in soldierly sentences proclaimed a series of inspiring and prophetic truths. We must be prepared to put armies of millions in the field and maintain them for several years.

Winston S. Churchill, speaking of Lord Kitchener, 1931[2]

on 5 June 1916, the ship carrying the field marshal, HMS *Hampshire*, hit a mine off the Orkney Islands and sank with almost all hands; Kitchener was drowned. The nation mourned.

OVERVIEW OF THE BRITISH ARMY

When Britain went to war in 1914, it had a small but highly trained army. The regular battalions available at home were enough to form six infantry divisions, each with around 15,000 men; each division was to have three infantry brigades, and each brigade in turn was to be composed of four infantry battalions. The six original divisions formed the British Expeditionary Force in 1914, the first four of them taking part in the retreat from Mons in 1914. The other two were present in France by September 1914. By the end of the war, the British Army had expanded from its original six to seventy-five infantry divisions, serving on three continents.

Ultimately, British and Commonwealth troops were to occupy 120 miles of the front, in the historically strategic zone that straddled the Belgo-French border, extending south deep into Picardy. Engaged from August 1914 at the Battle of Mons, the British Expeditionary Force grew in size and stature to become the backbone of the Allied effort in the closing months of 1918, with 5,399,563 empire troops employed on the Western Front alone. The vast majority of these were from the UK. But in 1915, the British Army had yet to come to its full strength, and was very much the junior partner to the French. This would affect the outcome of the campaigns during this difficult year.

THE COMMANDERS

Field Marshal Sir John French

Field Marshal French was the commander-in-chief of the British Expeditionary Force from 1914 to 1915. He was a cavalry commander during the Second Boer War of 1899–1902. As an experienced and senior soldier, French was appointed command of the British Expeditionary Force in August 1914. It was French that led the force into its position at Mons in 1914 – against the advice of Kitchener (and Haig), who suggested a position farther south – leading to an almost immediate retirement in the face of the German onslaught.

I WAS THERE

I have no more reserves. The only men I have left are the sentries at my gates. I will take them where the line is broken, and the last of the English will die fighting.

Sir John French, describing the First Battle of Ypres, October 1914[5]

DID YOU KNOW?

At the Battle of Le Cateau in 1914, Sir John French's orders to retire were ignored by General Sir Horrace Smith-Dorrien, commander of II Corps, who instead turned to fight. This action was to relieve pressure on the retiring British Expeditionary Force – but was to lose Smith-Dorrien his job.

Despite his name, Sir John's relationship with his French allies was fragile. He was placed in the difficult position of, on the one hand, acting as a subordinate ally to the more numerous and substantial French supporting General Joffre and, on the other, maintaining the independence of the British Expeditionary Force. He was forced into political debates that he would rather have steered clear of. Faced with demands from Joffre to support the French offensives in Artois, counterpoint to the offensives in the Champagne, Sir John was inclined to take the defensive. Despite this, and ordered to support the French at all costs, Sir John participated in the battles of Neuve Chapelle (in which there was a limited breakthrough), Aubers Ridge and Festubert during 1915.

I WAS THERE

I deeply regret the heavy casualties which were incurred in this battle, but in view of the great strength of the position, the stubborn defence of the enemy and the powerful artillery by which he was supported, I do not think they were excessive.

Sir John French, describing the Battle of Loos, November 1915

The Battle of Loos, in September 1915, would ultimately be French's undoing. Still holding on to the view that his armies should stand on the defensive until reinforced, he at first agreed to the battle and then shrank back from it. And it was Sir John's fateful decision to retain the reserves under his direct control that put strain on his fragile command. Held 15 miles from the battlefront, two new and inexperienced divisions were committed too late, putting intolerable strain on the commander of the First Army, Sir Douglas Haig. With failure to break through at Loos, and with French trying to gloss over the issues, Haig pushed for his removal, and eventually took Sir John's position as commander-in-chief of the British Expeditionary Force in December 1915. French returned to command British Home Forces in December 1915, overseeing the British armed response to the Irish Rebellion of 1916. He was made Lord Lieutenant of Ireland in May 1918, surviving an attempt on his life in December 1919.

Field Marshal Sir Douglas Haig

Sir Douglas Haig was born of a family of Scotch whisky distillers, and, unusually for generals of his day, had a university education, studying at Oxford. He did not attain his degree due to illness, but passing his exams made him eligible

I WAS THERE

To sum up the results of the fighting of these five days, on a front of over six miles, from the Briqueterie to La Boisselle, our troops had swept over the whole of the enemy's first and strongest system of defence, which he had done his utmost to render impregnable. They had driven him back over a distance of more than a mile, and had carried four elaborately fortified villages. The number of prisoners passed back at the close of the 5th July had already reached the total of ninety-four officers and 5,724 other ranks.

Sir Douglas Haig, referring to the opening of the Battle of the Somme, July 1916[5]

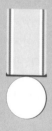

for Sandhurst. He saw service in India from 1888 to 1892, before entering the Staff College at Camberley.

Sir Douglas served in a variety of Victorian 'small wars' before being promoted to lieutenant general in 1910. Haig took control of Aldershot Command in 1912, which would ultimately form a large part of the British Expeditionary Force – I Corps – in August 1914. Haig and his men took part in the British Expeditionary Force's withdrawal from Mons in 1914, with I Corps eventually taking up its position at Ypres during the race for the sea at the end of that year, holding the line and ensuring that the city was not lost. In December 1914, I Corps was transformed into the First Army, again, with Haig in command.

The First Army had a major role to play in the campaigns of 1915. At Neuve Chapelle, it was Haig's army that took the offensive, supporting the synchronous French Artois and Champagne attacks that were intended to cut off the huge Noyon Salient. Haig would be back in action in Artois at Aubers Ridge in May, a battle with minimal effect; a renewed offensive to the south at Festubert later that month would have a similar effect. With Joffre still insisting that the British press the Germans in Artois, Loos was the next time that Haig would be called

I WAS THERE

Every position must be held to the last man: there must be no retirement. With our backs to the wall, and believing in the justice of our cause, each one of us must fight on until the end. The safety of our Homes and the Freedom of mankind alike depend on the conduct of each one of us at this critical moment.

Sir Douglas Haig, in the wake of Ludendorff's offensive, 1918°

upon to field his First Army in an offensive, although he would also express dissatisfaction about the open terrain. But the attack, albeit over 'unfavourable ground', would have to press ahead.

Haig, described as an 'incurable optimist' by some writers, often believed he could make a decisive breakthrough, but was less than articulate in inspiring confidence in this result. And although some writers have described Haig as a general rooted in tradition, fearful of new technology and clinging to cavalry tactics, the facts are that the general – later promoted to field marshal – embraced new weapons such as gas, at Loos in 1915, and tanks on the Somme. He also developed an ideal of all arms attacks that would prove successful in his 'forgotten victory' – the Battles of Hundred Days – that pushed the Germans back successively from the opening of the offensive on 8 August 1918. But it is the losses on the Somme (1916) and at Passchendaele (1917) that Haig is most associated with – and which have attracted his most virulent critics in recent decades. Haig and Lloyd George did not hit it off, and the Welshman severely criticised his commander-in-chief. Nevertheless, there was no one else able to do his job as well as he could, and Haig finished the war a national hero.

DID YOU KNOW?

Not without controversy, Haig's command has been discussed ever since, particularly his actions on the Somme (1916), and at Third Ypres (1917). Less discussed, at least until recently, have been his actions in leading his armies to decisive victory in 1918.

General Sir Edmund Allenby

Allenby had been commissioned into the army in 1882, having passed through Sandhurst. A cavalryman, he saw action in the Boer War and later served in a number of senior cavalry roles. With the outbreak of world war he was naturally given command of the Cavalry Division of the British Expeditionary Force as it left for France; the division would serve the British Expeditionary Force well in covering its retreat from Mons.

As the army expanded, so did Allenby's role. He was made commander of the Cavalry Corps, before relinquishing control of his horsemen to take command of V Corps, part of the Second Army in the Ypres Salient. Allenby was competent enough in this role and put in charge of the Third Army in October 1915, which was to see action at Gommecourt on the Somme in July 1916 – in an ill-fated diversion of the main attack – and at Arras in April 1917.

I WAS THERE

I entered the city officially at noon, December 11th, with a few of my staff, the commanders of the French and Italian detachments, the heads of the political missions, and the Military Attaches of France, Italy, and America. The procession was all afoot ... The population received me well.

Sir Edmund Allenby, entering Jerusalem, December 1917[7]

DID YOU KNOW?

Allenby was renowned for his imposing frame and bursts of violent temper, and this earned him the nickname 'the Bull'. Certainly his fellow officers felt the full force of this temperament.

However, neither impressed Haig, now commander-in-chief of the British Expeditionary Force, and although he was promoted to full general, Allenby was returned to England two months after the Arras attack.

With Lloyd George pushing for action on other fronts, Allenby's aggressive stance was considered to be perfect for Egypt; and it was in Egypt, as well as during his offensive against the Ottomans in Palestine, that Allenby made his name. Lloyd George demanded that Allenby be 'in Jerusalem by Christmas', taking the fight to the Ottomans. This he did, and Allenby entered the Holy City of Jerusalem, on foot, on 11 December. Given an independent command, 'the Bull' had achieved what he had failed to do in France and Flanders. But the demands of fighting on the Western Front deprived him, in a 'sideshow', of manpower resources: the Western Front had to come first. Standing on the defensive until September 1918, Allenby was then able to resume his pursuit of the Ottomans, inflicting a crushing defeat on them at Megiddo before capturing Damascus on 1 October. The Ottomans were beaten; by the end of that month they sued for peace. Allenby was promoted to field marshal in 1919.

FRANCE

FRANCE WAS THE senior Entente partner, and with its territories invaded and its borders violated, the French made strenuous efforts to expel the invaders and stay on the offensive.

THE LEADERS

Georges Clemenceau

Georges Clemenceau was the most influential French politician during the First World War, though he came late to power, having missed out on being president to Raymond Poincaré in 1913. Clemenceau had served as prime minister before, in 1907–10, and the old Republican was ardent in his opposition to trades unions and socialist politics.

DID YOU KNOW?

Georges Clemenceau was nicknamed *Le Tigre* – the Tiger – for his aggressive Republicanism; he also earned the title 'Father of Victory' after the war ended.

I WAS THERE

War is too serious a matter to leave to soldiers.

Georges Clemenceau, 1914[1]

DID YOU KNOW?

In 1919 Georges Clemenceau insisted that the Treaty of Versailles be signed in the same Hall of Mirrors at Versailles where, in 1871, Kaiser William I had proclaimed himself emperor of the unified Germany, following the defeat of France.

At the outbreak of war, Clemenceau was offered a position as justice minister under the then prime minister, Rene Viviani. Instead he decided to be an open critic, and edited a range of journals that sought to challenge the French approach to the war. In particular, he was a critic of Joseph Joffre, and also used his skills to censure the government openly. With France facing difficulties in the wake of Verdun and the failure of Nivelle's offensive in 1917 – an interval that led to widespread mutiny in the French Army – President Poincaré turned to his old rival to lead the government, in November 1917.

Clemenceau was committed to victory, even at the advanced age of 76. As the Allied line was severely pressed by Ludendorff's offensives in the spring of 1918, the opportunity came to cement in place one of Clemenceau's central ideas: a unified command. Until this point, the Allied leaders on the Western Front had acted independently, but with the Germans striking at the junction between the British and the French intending to cleave them apart, it was clear that a generalissimo was needed urgently. That man was General Ferdinand Foch, and the tide turned once again in favour of the Allies. With victory, Clemenceau was the main author of the Treaty of Versailles, his aggressive stance ensuring that the treaty was as punitive as possible.

OVERVIEW OF THE FRENCH ARMY

The French Army was composed mostly of men drawn from peasant stock, from the fields and villages of rural France. Of greatest importance to the people of France was its staggering defeat – as one of the most powerful military nations in the world – by the Prussians in 1871, during the Franco-Prussian War. The terms of the peace treaty with Prussia were harsh, and the loss of Alsace and Lorraine hard felt.

Post-war, the French Army was reorganised. To ensure that German aggression could be effectively countered, a series of forts were constructed that were designed to protect the frontiers – Verdun being one of these – and a huge conscript army was developed after the German model. Each soldier had to serve for five years to ensure continuity and to develop a system of reserves. French field artillery became the envy of many armies, with the 75mm field gun being recognised as the best quick-firing field gun of its day. Though this represented modern technology, the French soldiers were still dressed according to tradition: red trousers and blue coats reflective of the tricolour flag. This would change to a muted 'horizon blue' in 1915.

In 1914, the French could field forty-seven divisions – a body of 777,000 men, the vast majority of whom came from France, but 47,000 of whom hailed from the French colonial possessions in Africa and elsewhere. By the end of the war, the French had mobilised some 8 million men, almost half a million of whom were derived from the colonies. Greater reliance on artillery tactics also meant that greater numbers of the men were conscripted into the artillery, indicative of the changing face of the war. In 1917, in the wake of the failed Nivelle Offensive, the French Army suffered widespread mutinies. These mutinies, based most often on simple grievances, were quelled by Pétain, who listened carefully to demands and improved conditions. By 1918, the French were once more fighting fit.

THE COMMANDERS

General Joseph Jacques Césaire Joffre

General Joffre was the commander-in-chief of the French Army in the west. Joffre was a product of the *École Polytechnique* in Paris, and was to see through the siege of Paris during the Franco-Prussian War of 1870–71. But it was his actions as commander-in-chief of the French Army, an appointment from 1912 onwards, that were to cement his reputation. The appointment was not without controversy, however: Joffre had no direct experience of command at this level and had never served in a staff position. Nevertheless, with the painful experience of the defeat of 1871 still fresh, Joffre was committed to ensuring that the army was not defensive minded. In 1913, with Germany still a perceived threat, Joffre bought into Plan XVII – an idea developed by the equally pugnacious General Ferdinand Foch as a means of dealing with their strong western neighbours.

DID YOU KNOW?

Joffre was ruthless in dismissing senior officers who had not displayed sufficient resolve in the face of an efficient and capable enemy.

I WAS THERE

Everywhere the enemy has left on the field numerous wounded and a quantity of munitions. Everywhere we have made prisoners while gaining ground. Our troops bear witness to the intensity of the fight, and the means employed by the Germans in their endeavours to resist our élan. The vigorous resumption of the offensive has determined our success. Officers, non-commissioned officers, and men! You have all responded to my appeal; you have all deserved well of your country.

General Joseph Joffre, 11 September 1914

The plan required the invasion of Alsace-Lorraine, which had been taken from the French in the aftermath of the war of 1870–71.

With the outbreak of war seeing the development of the Schlieffen Plan in northern France, the flaws in Plan XVII were very much in evidence. However, it was Joffre who was able to muster his forces to take on the might of the advancing German Army while the French were reeling back from the German attempts to outflank Paris, ultimately saving the capital and the nation at the Battle of the Marne in 1914.

Joseph Joffre was committed to the offensive, and particularly the concept of simultaneous attacks on the German line in Artois and the Champagne, thereby hoping to eliminate the Noyon Salient, which was a huge elbow-like bulge in the line. He believed that there would be a breakthrough in this area; Joffre would not lose faith in this plan throughout 1915, despite the huge number of casualties. The failure of these campaigns would weaken Joffre's hold on the French command, his position further weakened by the titanic efforts of the German Army to break the line and 'bleed the French Army white' at Verdun in 1916.

Following both Verdun and the Somme Offensive of 1916, Joffre was promoted to Marshal of France, but was removed and replaced by the ill-fated Robert Nivelle on 13 December 1916.

General Ferdinand Foch

Ferdinand Foch is most often associated with the art of the offensive in the First World War. Born in the French Pyrenean town of Tarbes in 1851, he dreamt of becoming a soldier. He served briefly as a private in the disastrous Franco-Prussian War in 1870, joined the prestigious *École Polytechnique* and then went on to serve as a junior artillery officer. Rising through the ranks, Foch went on to join the War School in 1885. Foch so impressed that he returned as an instructor ten years later and ultimately became its director.

In 1911 Foch was placed in command of an infantry division and then, later, a corps. In August 1914, facing the lost province of Lorraine, Foch's XX Corps had an influential role in the Battle of Lorraine, enacting the French Plan XVII that was designed to punch into the German-held province. The French initially made rapid progress, but were soon in difficulties. With a German counter-attack, there was real danger that the French Second Army would be surrounded and trapped. It had to retreat. Only Foch's XX Corps stood its ground. This was truly in line with the French general's pugnacious approach.

I WAS THERE

My centre is giving way, my right is retreating, situation excellent, I am attacking.

General Ferdinand Foch to General Joseph Joffre, during the Battle of the Marne, 8 September 1914[10]

DID YOU KNOW?

It was at the War School that Foch developed his particular penchant for the offensive. He set out his ideals in his book *Des Principes de la Guerre* (*Principles of War*, 1903) which stressed the importance of the will of the commander to succeed and the importance of developing the offensive.

Foch soon rose to become General Joseph Joffre's deputy, in October 1914, commanding all the French forces in the north of the country. In this role he had control of the two offensives in Artois that would lead to large numbers of casualties and would confirm the difficulties of attacking the fortress that the Western Front had become.

Though Foch would experience success on the Somme in concert with the British, he fell from power when Joffre was replaced by Nivelle in 1917. The proponent of the offensive was relegated to a planning position, once more using his academic experience to play out strategic scenarios – one of which was the defeat of the Italian Army.

Foch's most significant role came at a time of crisis. In March to April 1918, the Allies were pushed back following General Ludendorff's offensives. Flustered, a single generalissimo was sought who could unite the multinational armies. With his experience, Foch was called to command. On 14 April, he became commander-in-chief of the Allied armies, co-ordinating their offensives of August 1918 that dealt the final death blows to the German armies, forcing them into a retreat that would be continuous for a 100 days. It was Foch that accepted the German surrender in the railway carriage at Compiègne on 11 November 1918; he was made Marshal of France in recognition of his achievements.

General Robert Georges Nivelle

Nivelle, born of an English mother and French father, had the benefit of a superior command of both languages, and with his confidence and energy was able to influence both British and French commanders when he rose to lead the French Army in 1916. Committed, in the French manner, to the doctrine of the offensive, he was also able to preach the twin ideals of an effective, rapid advance and limited casualties – based on his belief of the power of artillery.

Nivelle's wartime career opened in 1914, when he was the commander of an artillery regiment. His self-assured artillery tactics brought him to the fore, and he proved himself effective in the opening campaigns of the war; so effective, in fact, that he was promoted from colonel to general in October 1914. He rose to command

III Corps in 1915 and, ultimately, during the Battle of Verdun, the Second Army, taking over from the now-promoted General Pétain and acting as his subordinate. Verdun was Erich von Falkenhayn's mincing machine, with the French troops drawn into a war of attrition. Constructed of mutually supporting artillery forts, Verdun was a focal point for the German and French armed struggles: the loss of Fort Douaument was celebrated as a German victory – and mourned as a French loss. Nivelle's star was set to rise when, in October 1916, his innovation in using specialist creeping barrages to protect the infantry meant that Douaument was once more taken into French hands. At Verdun, he delivered: predicting success, he achieved it. Because of this, and his confidence, Nivelle was placed in charge of the French Army, replacing the ousted Joffre in December 1916.

DID YOU KNOW?

Pétain used the phrase '*On les aura!*' ('We'll get them!') in absolute confidence that the French would win out over the Germans at Verdun. However, it was his successor in command of the Second Army in the battle, General Nivelle, who finally uttered the words '*Ils ne passeront pas*' ('They shall not pass!').

In post, Nivelle planned an audacious attack in the Champagne region. Brimming with confidence, Nivelle made extravagant claims, buoyed by his successes. Using massed artillery, Nivelle fully expected to break through the German lines – or he would break off the attack. Nivelle's offensive opened on 16 April 1917, but the bombardment failed. The French suffered 120,000 casualties. Though there had been some gains, the claims made by the Frenchman could not be substantiated and he ended the offensive in the opening days. Nivelle's career was holed below the waterline – and the French Army went into mutiny. His old chief, Pétain, replaced him on 15 May, and put in place measures that would repair the damaged morale of the French Army. Nivelle was farmed out to Africa as commander-in-chief of the French Army there, and he was to take no further active service in the war.

General Henri Philippe Benoni Omer Pétain

Henri Philippe Pétain was a product of an agrarian tradition, born in rural France on 24 April 1856. Like many of his contemporaries, Pétain joined the French Army in the aftermath of the defeat of France during the Franco-Prussian War and rose slowly through the ranks to command an infantry regiment.

DID YOU KNOW?

Pétain had served in the influential War School as a professor, but his views ran counter to the prevailing doctrine of the offensive as promulgated by Foch, recognising that the power of modern weaponry favoured the defender, and he was not successful there.

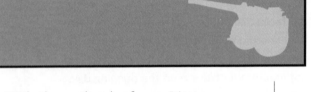

With the outbreak of war, Pétain was promoted to command a brigade and took part in Joffre's Artois offensive in 1915. His stock rose dramatically when he was ordered to stop the German offensive that was pulverising the fortress town of Verdun, a fortress that pushed out pugnaciously in the direction of the German lines. Here the defensively minded Pétain reorganised the front and instigated the transport supply columns that ground up the road that would become known as *La Voie Sacrée* – the sacred way. The general was respected by his men, and from this position he was able to instil nerve and discipline. Pétain stabilised the situation and Verdun and helped create its mythology: the strength of Verdun stood for the strength of the French nation.

The promotion of his subordinate, General Nivelle, had proven to be a costly mistake; so costly, in fact, that the failure of his much-heralded offensive of 1917 led to widespread mutinies in the French Army. With Nivelle sacked, there was no better man to step in as commander-in-chief than Pétain. The popular hero quickly re-established discipline in the mutinous army, communicating his intentions to his men directly and physically improving their living conditions. Though cautious, his approach rebuilt the army so that it could take part in the titanic battles of the autumn of 1918; battles that drove the Germans back continuously for 100 days. In the closing days of the war he was made Marshal of France, and would be tried for treason in 1945 for leading the puppet Vichy government.

DID YOU KNOW?

Pétain's mantra at Verdun, '*On les aura!*' ('We'll get them'), was transformed into one of the most successful slogans of the war, and came to personify the French soldier, the ordinary *poilu*.

RUSSIA

GERMANY FEARED THE might of the vast territory of the Russian Empire and its almost limitless resources. France was to be dispatched from the war quickly, before Russia was to be defeated.

THE LEADERS

Tsar Nicholas II

Nicholas II, 'emperor and autocrat of all the Russias', was the last Tsar of Russia and the head of state of the Russian Empire. He ruled from 1894 to his enforced abdication in 1917, and took an active role in the direction of not only the state, but also the Russian Army, serving as its commander after his cousin, the Grand Duke Nikolaevich, was relieved of his command. Under Nicholas' rule, Russia had suffered humiliating defeat in the Russo-Japanese War of 1904–05, widely held to be a blueprint for the world war that followed just ten years later. In its wake came a revolution in 1905 that was brutally put down, earning the Tsar a reputation for bloody oppression in some quarters.

DID YOU KNOW?

Nicholas II was first cousin to both Kaiser Wilhelm II of Germany and King George V of Britain.

I WAS THERE

In the days of the great struggle against the foreign enemies, who for nearly three years have tried to enslave our fatherland, the Lord God has been pleased to send down on Russia a new heavy trial. Internal popular disturbances threaten to have a disastrous effect on the future conduct of this persistent war.

Nicholas II, abdication statement, 15 March 1917[11]

And it was the Tsar who ordered a general mobilisation on 31 July 1914, an act that overheated the already tinder-dry atmosphere of pre-war Europe. Though Nicholas II had sent a telegram to his cousin, Wilhelm II, asking for arbitration between Austria-Hungary and Serbia via The Hague, the German demand for demobilisation was unrealistic and peace passed to war. With war, the Tsar became remote from his people, spending much time away at the front, while unrest grew. Increasing casualties and food shortages led to unrest, which was put down by force, and demand grew for his deposition. The Tsar finally abdicated in March 1917, the Provisional Government briefly taking the reins. It was too late for Russia, and for the Tsar and his family. With the collapse of the Provisional Government, Russia, now under Bolshevik rule, sued for peace. The Tsar's family were taken prisoner and executed in Tobolsk, in the Urals.

OVERVIEW OF THE RUSSIAN ARMY

At the outbreak of the war, Tsar Nicholas II appointed his cousin, Grand Duke Nicholas, as commander-in-chief. On mobilisation, the Russian Army could boast some 15.8 million men in uniform – two-fifths of the male population of service age – and supported some 115 infantry and thirty-eight cavalry divisions. A combined total of some seventy-eight infantry and twenty-nine cavalry divisions faced the Central Powers of Germany and Austria-Hungary.

No other nation would mobilise as many men in prosecution of the war. But all was not well. Ensuring that this impressive number of men each had a rifle and bayonet was a significant challenge to the Russians, whose economy was not capable of gearing up to maximum war effort. Russia was completely unprepared for war, its armies ill-equipped. While Russia headed the tables in the supply of men, it was very much at the bottom when it came to military expenditure. Russia expended some 1.8 billion dollars a year on the supply of their military during the First World War, but Germany, Britain and even the United States spent at least twice as much on their military consumables. This deficit would have a net effect on the soldiers at the front, many of whom would have to do without a rifle of their own.

THE COMMANDERS

Grand Duke Nikolai Nikolaevich

Grand Duke Nikolai had impeccable imperial connections within the Romanov-led Russian Empire. After all, Nikolai Nikolaevich was the grandson of Tsar Nicholas I, and first cousin of the reigning Tsar, Nicholas II. The grand duke was educated as a soldier in the Russian School of Military Engineers, graduating in 1872. Though serving in the Russo-Turkish War of 1877–78, for the most part he was a man who was devoted to staff work and in the reorganisation and development of training and tactics. From commander of the St Petersburg Military District in 1905, Nikolaevich rose to command the whole of the Russian Army in the field in 1914. This was unexpected, but may have been a move to prevent the Tsar himself leading his men.

The year 1914 would prove disastrous for the Russians. With the Russian territory so vast, communication was difficult, so the grand duke was faced with delegation of responsibility to his commanders, on a large scale, although he was still nominally in charge. After some early successes in East Prussia, and against the Austro-Hungarians in Galicia, the Russian Army was continually under threat, the successes reversed.

DID YOU KNOW?

Nikolaevich's reforms, particularly during his service as inspector general of cavalry from 1895, helped redefine and develop the Russian armed forces in the field, though for the most part they lagged behind those of the other armies.

The close of 1914 saw the disastrous defeat at Tannenberg, his commander, Samsonov, taking his life rather than facing the Tsar. As the man in charge, Nikolaevich was removed from command in 1915 and sent to the Caucasus to command the developing war against the Ottomans. Here, with the successful general Nikolai Yudenich in place, his reputation was restored.

With his removal, the Tsar himself took command, with disastrous consequences. The same difficulties that had plagued Nikolaevich affected the Tsar. His command was weakened and his grip on the country almost lost. The grand duke advised his cousin to introduce reforms to save his reputation, leading to a recommendation for abdication. Before all was lost, the Tsar once more attempted to put the grand duke in charge, but this was unacceptable to Georgy Lvov and his new Provisional Government. Nikolaevich was dismissed and went into exile in 1919.

General Alexander Samsonov

Alexander Samsonov is the general most associated with the tragedy of defeat, committing suicide after the disastrous Battle of Tannenberg, fought between 26 and 30 August 1914. The battle was intended to cut off the German Eighth Army south-west of Königsburg in East Prussia; but it soon developed into a major defeat, with the loss of 92,000 Russians captured and 78,000 killed. Just 10,000 escaped: the Russian Second Army was decimated. With such a major defeat, the Russians were in disarray and the Entente Powers were seriously threatened.

Samsonov joined the 12th Hussars as a junior officer, serving in the Russo-Turkish War of 1877–78. He rose to a cavalry command in the Boxer Rebellion of 1900 and the Russo-Japanese War of 1904–05, and was called to command the Russian Second Army upon mobilisation of the Tsar's army in 1914. It was in this role, alongside General Paul von Rennenkampf (a rival following a dispute at the Battle of Mukden in 1905) of the First Army, that he was given orders to invade East Prussia.

Samsonov commenced his invasion, in the south-west of East Prussia, carefully, while his rival attacked from the north. Communication between the two rivals was poor, and

Samsonov's army was soon surrounded by the German Eighth Army between 26 and 30 August 1914. The defeat was total: of an army of 150,000 just 10,000 escaped capture. Vast amounts of Russian war booty were returned to Germany, reputedly in sixty trains. Horrified at the scale of the defeat, Samsonov shot himself, and his body was never found.

General Nikolai Iudovich Ivanov

General Nikolai Ivanov commenced his military career in the artillery. Like many of the other Russian military commanders, his first taste of action was during the Russo-Turkish War of 1877–78, and he went on to a command in the Russian Imperial Guards Artillery, and subsequently became commandant of the artillery fortress of Kronstadt. Later, as commander of the Kiev Military District, he oversaw mobilisation of forces at the outbreak of war.

Campaigning in 1914, Ivanov achieved staggering successes against the Austro-Hungarians in Galicia. Conrad von Hötzendorf opened an offensive against Ivanov's forces in August 1914 in the hope that he could steal a march on the stronger Russians. But von Hötzendorf's advance in the north was outwitted by Ivanov's thrust in the south, at Lemberg. His flank threatened, von Hötzendorf was pushed back in disarray, and Ivanov pushed his front deep into Galicia and the Carpathian mountains. With Tannenberg an absolute disaster for the Russians in East Prussia, Ivanov's success farther south was a sweeter pill to swallow.

However, Ivanov was unable to build on his success. Outnumbering the Austro-Hungarians, his natural caution counted against him. And when General August von Mackensen pushed back at the Russians in the sharply focused Golice–Tarnów Offensive of May 1915, Ivanov's forces were routed, the gains of 1914 lost. The Russian Third Army was destroyed, the fortress of Przemyśl, which had fallen to the Russians after a five-month siege in March 1915, was recaptured in early June and the Russians were forced out of Galicia. Ivanov was dismissed and his command given to General Aleksei Brusilov. Still retaining imperial favour, however, Ivanov was given the position of military advisor to the Tsar – though any views he might have held were ignored by the Chief of Staff, Mikael Alexseev. In revolutionary Russia, Ivanov's White Army was defeated in the Russian Civil War; Ivanov himself, an ardent supporter of the Tsar to the end, died of typhoid in 1919.

DID YOU KNOW?

At the end of the Ivanov's Battle of Galicia, fought in 1914, the Austro-Hungarian Empire had lost some 324,000 men, 130,000 of them prisoners. The Russian had also surrounded the fortress city of Przemyśl, committing it to an extended siege that would eventually lead to its loss.

General Aleksei Alekseevich Brusilov

General Aleksei Alekseevich Brusilov received his education in the Imperial Corps of Pages in St Petersburg and, like so many of his contemporaries, served with distinction in the Russo-Turkish War, being decorated numerous times and rising through the ranks to reach general in 1906.

Commanding an army in 1914, Brusilov was to prove himself highly successful, and during Ivanov's offensive helped stove in the Austro-Hungarian front, driving them back some 93 miles. Through this he helped to build his commander's early positive reputation as a military commander. But with the German-led fight-back at Gorlice–Tarnów in 1915, Brusilov had to conform to the retirement of the Russian

I WAS THERE

If there remain any Germans still hopeful for their cause, let them realise that today, when the Central Powers have lost the initiative and are finding a difficulty in refilling their ranks, Russia has not yet reached the zenith of her power.

Aleksei Brusilov, in the wake of his offensive, 1916[12]

DID YOU KNOW?

Brusilov was known as a thinker and a man who was capable of detailed planning, but who was flexible enough to exploit tactical success. For these reasons, he was capable of turning the tide of the war in this region in favour of the Russians – albeit briefly. His approach was highly influential, and would be reused by the Germans in planning for their offensives in the west in 1918.

armies. With Ivanov sacked in the wake of the withdrawal, it was natural that Brusilov would be confirmed as his successor, which happened in March 1916.

While the Russian thrusts had seen the use of narrow fronts with indifferent artillery preparation, Brusilov insisted that future offensives should be on a broad front, with several points of attack to confuse the enemy, short lightning bombardments in support of men brought up as close as possible to the enemy and a strategic reserve ready to join with the front troops to exploit success.

On 4 June 1916, Brusilov put his ideas to the test in an offensive that opened in Galicia with staggering success. Concentrating forty divisions on a 300-mile front, his accurate bombardment took the Austrians by surprise, and his infiltration tactics left them reeling. The success of the offensive meant that the Russians were in danger of being over-extended, taking the city of Lutsk and pushing on as far as they could. The offensive continued on into September, reaching the Carpathian Mountains – over the ground lost by Ivanov the previous year. The campaign petered out as the Russians were forced to redeploy troops to bolster their new ally, Romania, which was persuaded to join the Entente Powers in the wake of Brusilov's success. The Austro-Hungarians were mostly a spent force, losing some 1.5 million men, and the Austrians abandoned hope that they could defeat the Italians.

In May 1917, Brusilov was given command of the whole Russian Army, overseeing the final Russian offensive of the war – the Kerensky Offensive of July 1917 – ordered by the Minister for War of the Provisional Government set up after the Tsar had abdicated. The offensive was marked by a highly co-ordinated artillery bombardment. However, although there were successes, the Russian troops were unable to maintain the pressure and morale began to crumble. On 19 July, the Germans and

Austro-Hungarians counter-attacked, and the Russians were forced into full retreat. Brusilov was replaced by General Kornilov in August 1917.

ITALY

ITALY JOINED THE Entente Powers through the secret Treaty of London, signed on 28 April 1915, in which Italy renounced her former ties to Germany and Austria-Hungary, and agreed to take offensive action against them in return for Austrian territory.

OVERVIEW OF THE ITALIAN ARMY

The Italian Army was fed by conscription that had been introduced in 1907, after the German model; yet it was imperfect, and the training given to recruits was far from ideal or universal. With 300,000 troops in the Italian Army in 1912, there was still a distinct lack of trained men and non-commissioned officers. In July 1914, Luigi Cadorna became the Chief of Staff of the Italian Army, and while the Italian Government openly declared its intentions to remain neutral, Cadorna prepared for war against the Austro-Hungarians. Following a secret meeting with Britain in April 1915, the Italians agreed to enter the war on the side of the Entente Powers.

Though Cadorna had prepared himself and his armies, by the spring of 1915, he had thirty-six infantry and four cavalry divisions at his disposal. The Alpine front with Austria represented some of the most inhospitable terrain in the world, and as such this was held on the defensive, with siege tactics being paramount. Here the experienced mountain troops of both sides struggled to gain the upper hand and maintain some ascendancy – not easy given the Austrians had, for the most part, the high ground. More accessible to the Italians was the open plain of the Isonzo, which would be the scene of successive battles against the Austrians, all too often unsupported by adequate artillery.

THE COMMANDERS

General Luigi Cadorna

Cadorna entered the Turin Military Academy at the age of 15. Graduating as a second lieutenant, he became an artillery officer and took an active part in the occupation of Rome in 1870, which saw the unification of Italy. Cadorna gradually rose through the ranks; committed to the doctrine of the offensive, the general had written on the topic and was close to retirement in 1915.

General Cadorna opened the war against the Austrians and launched successive offensives along the Isonzo valley that were intended to allow the Italians to enter Austro-Hungary and march on Trieste. All of these offensives failed through poor artillery preparation and general weariness of the troops called upon to make mass attacks against a determined enemy. Eleven consecutive attacks were launched against the Austrian lines on the Isonzo alone. But perhaps the defining moment in Cadorna's military career was when a combined Austro-Hungarian and German offensive struck at Caporetto on the Isonzo River on 24 October 1917, pushing on all the way to the Piave River and threatening the security of the whole of Italy; some 275,000 Italians surrendered in the offensive. Cadorna himself fled the battle, abandoning the Italian Army to its fate.

Bolstering their weaker ally in the wake of the defeat, the British and French sent eleven divisions to support them – and insisted on Cadorna's dismissal. Once the line was stabilised under General Armando Diaz, the Italian Army was again in a fit state to face its enemies.

DID YOU KNOW?

Cadorna's reputation as a martinet stuck with him throughout his career: he dismissed as many as 217 officers from their posts during the war and one in every seventeen Italian soldiers faced some form of military charge. In all, some 750 soldiers were executed, the highest number in any army.

Though he was appointed Italian representative to the Treaty of Versailles, Cadorna was castigated in a post-war inquiry into Caporetto.

General Armando Diaz

Armando Diaz commenced his military career as a student of the Military Academy of Turin, graduating to become an artillery officer. Diaz saw military action in the Italo-Turkish War of 1911–12, and was ultimately promoted to the rank of major general in 1914. With Cadorna, he contributed materially to the creation of a more focused Italian Army in preparation for the participation in the First World War, and served initially as Cadorna's Chief of Operations. In May 1915, he went on to become both divisional and corps commanders in the field, assisting the chief in his victories over the Austrians in August 1916, at Carso and Gorizia. But it was the overwhelming disaster at Caporetto that propelled Diaz into the limelight: with Cadorna's defeat and his harsh treatment of troops, a new man was needed, and that was Diaz.

Stabilising the army, Diaz successfully repelled the Austrian attack on June 1918, and mounted a counter-offensive. Although at first he was reluctant to carry out a major offensive, he was pressed to do so by the Italian Prime Minister Vittorio Orlando. As such, Diaz opened

I WAS THERE

The remnants of what was one of the world's most powerful armies are climbing back in hopelessness and chaos up the valleys from which they had descended with boastful confidence.

General Armando Diaz, Army Chief of Staff, Bollettino della Vittoria, 1918[13]

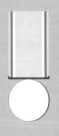

an attack on the Austro-Hungarians at Vittorio Veneto and ultimately presided over a decisive victory on 3 November 1918 – a defeat that summoned the end for the Austro-Hungarian forces. Diaz issued his famous final address to the army to mark the occasion a day later, a speech, the *Bollettino della Vittoria*, that has since been memorialised across Italy.

DID YOU KNOW?

Diaz's offensive at Vittorio Veneto was launched with fifty-seven divisions, and succeeded in the destruction of the Austro-Hungarians. Diaz was rewarded with the title of *duca della vittoria* (duke of victory) in 1921.

UNITED STATES
OF AMERICA

THE UNITED STATES of America joined the Entente Powers – as a so-called 'Associated Power' – on 6 April 1917, in the wake of the German readoption of unrestricted submarine warfare, which threatened American neutrality and freedom of the seas.

THE LEADERS

President Woodrow Wilson

Woodrow Wilson was a Democrat who served as the twenty-eighth President of the United States, from 1913 to 1921, straddling the war years. In his first term of office, Wilson was happy to campaign on the platform of 'keeping America out of the war'. However, on re-election for his second term of office in 1916, he was faced with the resumption of submarine warfare, which had seen the *Lusitania* sunk with the loss of a great many American lives in 1915. With Germany declaring that no neutral ships would be safe in the war zone – as well as making misguided overtures towards Mexico to attack the United States – Wilson was left no choice but to enter the conflict on the side of the Entente Powers, asking Congress to declare war on 5 April 1917.

I WAS THERE

What we demand in this war, therefore, is nothing peculiar to ourselves. It is that the world be made fit and safe to live in; and particularly that it be made safe for every peace-loving nation which, like our own, wishes to live its own life, determine its own institutions, be assured of justice and fair dealing by the other peoples of the world, as against force and selfish aggression.

President Woodrow Wilson, speaking in the US Congress, 8 January 1918[14]

DID YOU KNOW?

Woodrow Wilson gave a speech on Flag Day, 14 June 1917 (the anniversary of the adoption of the American flag), which led to a widespread wave of anti-German sentiment in the USA.

Wilson introduced the draft to staff the army and ensured that America had sufficient funds to fight the war – and sufficient industrial muscle to win it. Famously, Wilson issued a statement in January 1918 that was to set out 'fourteen points' for peace, recognising freedom of peoples and the seas, and the rights of free trade and self-determination of the populations of the crumbling empires of Europe. Though many Allied leaders were sceptical, they respected Wilson's high aims, which went on to inform the Treaty of Versailles, formally ending the war in July 1919.

OVERVIEW OF THE US ARMY

On the outbreak of war, the United States had only a small standing army of around 100,000 men, totally inadequate to prosecute a war in the field. To ensure that manpower would meet the needs of service, the Americans introduced the Selective Service Act on 18 May 1917: a law that allowed American men to be drafted into the army. This thereby allowed for the creation of a national army that would supply some 4 million men, with the American Expeditionary Force taking almost 2 million of these to serve alongside their European allies in France.

It took some time for American men to be trained into battle readiness. They were equipped with their own uniforms, webbing and rifles, but drew upon the experience of their allies, who supplied the American Expeditionary Force with artillery pieces, tanks, steel helmets and gas masks. The first offensives fought by the Americans in France were in relatively quiet sectors, and then alongside Australian troops at Hamel in July 1918; the first all-American offensive was at St Mihiel in September, and then in the Meuse-Argonne. With General Pershing pushing for an aggressive stance against the Germans, the Americans were engaged fighting the Germans on the last day of the war.

THE COMMANDERS

General John Joseph Pershing

Born in rural Missouri, John Pershing's first military assignment was as a second lieutenant in the 6th Cavalry. He took part in a number of operations against the Native American Lakota people, before being promoted to command a troop of the 10th Cavalry.

Pershing would see further combat experience in the Spanish-American War of 1898, as well as in the Philippines in 1903; as an observer he saw first-hand the nature of modern warfare in the Russo-Japanese War of 1904–05. In 1915, he commanded an expedition to capture the Mexican revolutionary general Pancho Villa, who had raided New Mexico in search of military supplies. The US entry into the war in 1917 placed Pershing in position to command an American Expeditionary Force to France. The US Army of the day consisted of just 25,000 men, so Pershing was faced with the task of raising an effective force of at least 500,000, training them, equipping them and leading them in the field.

I WAS THERE

Lafayette, we are here.

General John Pershing, pausing at the tomb of French
hero the Marquis de Lafayette, a general of the American
Revolutionary War, 4 July 1917 [15]

DID YOU KNOW?

The 10th Cavalry was a segregated regiment of black troopers – known to the Native Americans as 'buffalo soldiers' – led by white officers. Not overly popular with his cadets at West Point, Pershing was known to them as 'Black Jack', which was then a hostile nickname referring to his 10th Cavalry command.

Pershing was unbending in his belief that American troops would not normally serve under foreign command, though they took part in the Battle of Hamel under British control as a means of gathering experience and he assigned black segregated divisions – the 92nd and 93rd – to French command. By August 1918, the US First Army was ready to take fully to the field, and did so at the Battle of St Mihiel, near Verdun, with success. Required to fit in with the wishes of the Allied generalissimo, Marshal Foch, the American Expeditionary Force was next in action in the Meuse-Argonne as part of the Allied grand strategy. Here, however, Pershing showed his inexperience by deploying frontal assaults with relatively weak artillery support. Though Pershing had been scornful of his allies' efforts in prosecuting trench warfare for so long, his troops were to experience it for themselves, with heavy losses. Ultimately, the US general was keen to ensure that the Germans were beaten in the field, and viewed the armistice with some suspicion: he ordered his men to keep fighting – even on the last day of the war. Pershing returned home a hero, and was promoted to the highest rank ever held by an American military officer – General of the Armies – by Congress.

PART 2

THE CENTRAL POWERS

GERMANY

GERMANY WAS A powerful military nation, and had been so since the defeat of France in 1871. She was the senior partner in the Central Powers.

THE LEADERS

Kaiser Wilhelm II

Kaiser Wilhelm II was the Emperor of Germany and the King of Prussia from 1888. Militaristic, within two years the Kaiser had dismissed the wily Chancellor Otto von Bismarck, and embarked upon a campaign to expand the German armed forces that was to destabilise the delicate power balance across Europe. He was particularly keen to build a navy that would challenge the Royal Navy of Britian – and as a consequence his intentions were viewed with great suspicion. His relationship with Britain was variable, and supporting the Boers in the South African War did nothing to improve his popularity. On the assassination of the Archduke Franz Ferdinand, Kaiser Wilhelm was out of the country and events spiralled out of his control. However, the Austrians – an ally of Germany – had been handed a 'blank cheque' by the Germans, who agreed to support them come what may; there was no turning back once nations started to mobilise.

I WAS THERE

A monarch who wishes war and prepares it in such a way that he can suddenly fall upon his neighbours — a task requiring long secret mobilisation preparations and concentration of troops — does not spend months outside his own country. My enemies, in the meantime, planned their preparations for an attack.

Kaiser Wilhelm II, discussing the opening of the war, 1922[16]

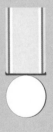

I WAS THERE

You will be home before the leaves have fallen from the trees.

Kaiser Wilhelm II, addressing his troops, August 1914[17]

Throughout the war, the Kaiser acted as the titular head of the army, though the Chief of Staff was the man who exercised the power. When von Hindenburg took over from Falkenhayn in this position, the Kaiser's power was eroded even more. Following the failure of the *Kaiserschlacht* – the Kaiser's battle against the Western Allies – in spring 1918, the tide of the war had turned against the Germans. With the Allies counter-attacking in August 1918, defeat was inevitable, and the Kaiser was forced to abdicate on 9 November 1918. He would live out the rest of his days in exile in the Netherlands.

OVERVIEW OF THE GERMAN ARMY

The Imperial German Army, the *Kaiserliches Heer or Reichsheer*, was formed in the wake of the Franco-Prussian War of 1871, and was composed of the armies of the numerous states that made up the German Empire. Dominant in this was the strong state of Prussia. The Prussian Army was to lead in all military aspects, co-ordinating matters with the other non-confederation states of Bavaria, Württemberg and Saxony. Each possessed semi-autonomous military contingents with their own identity and customs.

It was through the General Staff that the Prussian Army system of excellence in leadership and organisation was maintained. The Imperial German Army in peacetime was divided into eight army inspectorates, with the Bavarians maintaining their own independent structure. At the outbreak of war, the inspectorates formed the command structure of field armies, and by 1918, these had grown to form nineteen armies in the field. Armies were further organised into army groups, composed of several armies. In turn, these armies would be divided into army corps.

In common with the British Army, in the German Army the division was a basic tactical formation. At the outbreak of war, there were forty-two regular divisions in the Prussian Army (including four Saxon divisions and two Württemberg divisions), as well as six divisions contributed by the semi-independent Bavarian Army. All would be mobilised for war, and there would be additional manpower in the form of *Landwehr*, consisting of troops that had completed their formal period of engagement with the regular forces. The *Landwehr* brigades were organised into divisions, and there would be replacement (*Ersatz*) units made from home guard (*Landstürm*). By the end of the war, 251 divisions had been formed in the German Army.

THE COMMANDERS

General Helmuth Johannes von Moltke

Helmuth Johannes von Moltke was a descendant of an old, aristocratic family of soldiers; he was destined to become an officer in the Prussian Army.

During the Franco-Prussian War of 1870–71, Moltke served with distinction before attending the Prussian Military Academy, and finally the General Staff in 1880. In 1882 he became personal adjutant to his uncle, Moltke the Elder, then Chief of the General Staff. Following his uncle's death in 1891, the younger Moltke became aide-de-camp to Wilhelm II, and ultimately became part of the emperor's inner circle. In 1906 he succeeded Alfred von Schlieffen as commander-in-chief of the General Staff, and in doing so became the most powerful army officer in Germany.

DID YOU KNOW?

Moltke the Younger was actually the nephew of Helmut Carl Bernhard von Moltke, Prussia's strategic mastermind during the German Wars of Unification.

I WAS THERE

Uncle Helmuth thinks that there might be war starting soon; just because everyone has been preparing for it for so long. Huge arsenals like this are always dangerous, but he also sees no necessity for war.

Dorothy Rose Innes, Moltke's niece, in a letter to her parents, 1912 [18]

In August 1914, influenced by Wilhelm II, Moltke made several changes to the Schlieffen Plan – the plan to invade France (via neutral Belgium) and knock it out of the war before Russia could come into the fight. One of his changes was to weaken the right wing of the German Army in order to strengthen the left, defending Alsace-Lorraine against the French invasion. Whilst Schlieffen had been willing to sacrifice some German territory in the short run in order to destroy the French Army, the younger Moltke refused to run the same risk. Moltke further weakened the Schlieffen Plan by unnecessary troop movements, reassigning a massive 250,000 men from the right-wing assault before finally abandoning the plan altogether.

Due to constant clashes and pressure from his superiors, the general's health broke down and, on 25 October 1914, he was succeeded by Erich von Falkenhayn. On 18 June 1916, after giving a speech at the funeral of General Colmar von der Goltz, he suffered a stroke that killed him instantly.

General Erich von Falkenhayn

Erich von Falkenhayn was born into an old aristocratic family in Graudenz, Prussia. Joining the army at an early age, von Falkenhayn acted as a military instructor in China from 1899, seeing action with the multinational force that opposed the Boxer Rebellion in 1900. His experience was valuable, and von Falkenhayn continued to serve with the General Staff, before being appointed Minister for War of the Prussian state.

It was in this role that von Falkenhayn clashed with the Chief of Staff, Helmuth von Moltke; with the failure of the Schlieffen Plan in August 1914, and the defeat of the Marne, Moltke was held responsible and was replaced with his rival in September, who became Chief of the Imperial General Staff. He served initially in both roles, until giving up the War Ministry in February 1915. Von Falkenhayn was widely considered to be cautious, inclined to the defensive. While this meant that he was often reluctant to commit resources to any one of the developing fronts, it also meant that bold actions – especially in the wide, open spaces of the Eastern Front – were often not taken soon enough, despite the release of troops gaining results.

DID YOU KNOW?

Attributed to von Falkenhayn is the concept of 'bleeding the French Army white' at the significant border fortress town of Verdun – the very essence of attrition.

DID YOU KNOW?

The Romanians entered the war on the Allied side in the wake of the success of the Brusilov Offensive. In 1916, von Falkenhayn presided over the complete defeat of the ill-prepared Romanian Army, entering Bucharest in December.

His caution in the east may have been clouded by his view that the real war was to be fought in the west. The offensive most associated with von Falkenhayn is the attack at Verdun in February 1916 – a battle that would become closely associated with the concept of battles of attrition. Hoping to draw the French into Verdun, his concept was to destroy them in detail, through the intensity of artillery fire and infantry assault. Staggering losses were felt on both sides, and though the capability of the French Army was reduced, so was that of the Germans. The concept failed, and Verdun, forever associated with von Falkenhayn, is regarded as one of the most costly battles in history. The German commander was replaced by his vocal rival, Paul von Hindenburg, in August 1916; sidelined, von Falkenhayn was sent to Transylvania to face the Romanians and, after their defeat, was dispatched to Mesopotamia in support of the Ottomans, and then on to Palestine in early 1917. Von Falkenhayn was unable to halt the advance of Allenby, and was defeated at Gaza at the close of October 1917. He was relieved in February 1918, sent to command an army in Lithuania, in obscurity.

Field Marshal Paul von Hindenburg

Paul von Hindenburg – more properly Paul von Beneckendorff und von Hindenburg – casts an imposing shadow over the Great War. Educated as a soldier from an early age, he became an officer in 1866 – in time to serve in the Austro-Prussian War – and later fought in the Franco-Prussian War of 1870–71. With these experiences, von Hindenburg joined the General Staff in 1905.

By the outbreak of war in 1914, von Hindenburg had already been retired for three years, but he was recalled to the army by Helmuth von Moltke. Very quickly, in August 1914 as commander of East Prussia, he built a significant reputation in the east, when he emphatically defeated the numerically superior Russian Army under General Samsonov at Tannenberg. Promoted, he was made commander-in-chief of the German armies in the east in September 1914, having a significant role in developing the war of the Eastern Front.

DID YOU KNOW?

Powerfully built, Field Marshal von Hindenburg became a totemic figure in Germany: a 12m-high wooden statue of the general was constructed in Berlin, and visitors paid for the opportunity to strike a symbolic iron nail home into its bulk.

Von Hindenburg developed a close relationship with his Chief of Staff, Erich Ludendorff, and together the two generals were able to achieve much against the Russians, defeating them at the Battle of the Masurian Lakes a week after Tannenberg – and achieving a second victory there in 1915. Von Hindenburg's reputation became as solid as his imposing figure, though at odds with the Chief of Staff, Erich von Falkenhayn, who was committed to the war in the west. Von Falkenhayn's ill-fated and costly offensive against the French at Verdun cost him his job – and saw his rival, now a field marshal, elevated to take it in August 1916. Not surprisingly, von Hindenburg took his right-hand man, Ludendorff, as quartermaster general.

Under von Hindenburg and Ludendorff, the Allied assaults of 1917 were repulsed and the Russians and Romanians defeated; in 1918, Germany went on to the offensive, attacking the western Allies at their weakest points

DID YOU KNOW?

From 1916 until the end of the war, von Hindenburg and Ludendorff ran the country in a virtual dictatorship, with Kaiser Wilhelm II a simple figurehead.

and causing the line to bulge. It did not break, however, and, with the Allies pushing back, Germany was defeated. Von Hindenburg survived with his reputation intact; he retired from the army in 1919, though did not resign from his post. He was there to read the abdication of the Kaiser.

General Erich Ludendorff

Erich Ludendorff developed a flair for mathematics in childhood, before being commissioned into the infantry in 1883, eventually joining the General Staff in 1894. Working closely with Alfred von Schlieffen, it was Ludendorff who was responsible for mobilisation, and he worked on the Schlieffen Plan itself, which would have an important influence on the opening campaign of the war. Ludendorff was a committed military man, devoted to his role; this made him difficult to know and like.

On the outbreak of war in 1914, Ludendorff was deputy to von Bülow, commanding the German Second Army. Charged with attacking the modern Belgian fortress of Liège – vital in permitting the free flow of the Schlieffen Plan – Ludendorff was faced with taking actual field command and reducing the fortification in the face of stiff resistance, which he did with aplomb. As the German invasion of the west continued, Ludendorff was sent with Paul von Hindenburg to resist the Russian push to capture East Prussia. The two men, working closely together, inflicted a great defeat on the Russians at Tannenberg, and were able to follow this up with victories that visited great losses on the Russian military. It was not surprising, then, that when von Hindenburg was sent to replace von Falkenhayn as the Chief of Staff, Ludendorff would accompany him, adopting the title 'quartermaster general'. It was in this role that Ludendorff directed the war in train with von Hindenburg, in a virtual dictatorship. It was Ludendorff who was the brains behind the partnership, using his organisational and mathematical skills.

I WAS THERE

August 8th was the black day of the German Army in the history of this war.

General Erich Ludendorff, referring to the first day of the Battle of Amiens, 1919[13]

With troops moved to the west, Ludendorff had high hopes for the German Spring Offensives of 1918. When these failed, his iron grip on affairs faltered, authority was passed back from von Hindenburg and himself to the Kaiser, and a negotiated peace was wavered over. Ultimately, he was forced to resign and, with the armistice, left the country for Scandinavia. In the immediate aftermath of the war, he wrote that the army had been 'stabbed in the back' by the civilian government, and he turned to the right for political solace.

DID YOU KNOW?

General Erich Ludendorff is a significant figure. Although in the shadow of Paul von Hindenburg, it is probable that Ludendorff provided the brains behind many of the pair's most significant victories on the Eastern Front and, later in the war, acted to direct German strategic aims.

AUSTRIA-HUNGARY

AUSTRIA-HUNGARY WAS A multinational amalgam of states, and had been bound together with Germany in a military alliance since 1879.

THE LEADERS

Kaiser Franz Josef I

Franz Josef was the Emperor of the Austro-Hungarian Empire for sixty-eight years and had seen his country's fortunes wax and wane, falling from a position of leading the German Confederation of States in the 1860s to a point where Austria had to recognise the importance of Hungary in the dual monarchy. Still, the need for protection against Russia was significant, given the power shift in the Balkans following the defeat of the Ottomans in 1879. This led to the creation of Bulgaria, and the increasing growth and influence of Serbia, Montenegro and Romania – principalities that would grow into kingdoms in the earliest years of the twentieth century. In 1908, jealous of the shifting scenes in the Balkans, Austria-Hungary annexed Bosnia. This added to the instability of the region, and ultimately led to war, when Franz Josef's heir to the throne, Franz Ferdinand, was murdered on the streets of Sarajevo on 28 June 1914.

DID YOU KNOW?

Franz Josef's sixty-eight-year reign is one of the longest in the history of Europe.

Though Franz Josef was shocked by the severity of the ultimatum sent to the Serbians in the wake of the assassination, he did not interfere with the views of his Foreign Minister and Chief of Staff, Conrad von Hötzendorf. Franz Josef stood by as Europe descended into war. The old emperor did not see the war out: he died in November 1916 and was replaced by Kaiser Karl I.

THE COMMANDERS

Field Marshal Franz Conrad von Hötzendorf

Franz Conrad von Hötzendorf was commissioned into the army as a lieutenant in a rifle (Feldjäger) regiment in 1871, before joining the Imperial War School in Vienna, with intent to join the General Staff – which he did five years later. Like many contemporaries, study of recent campaigns convinced him that attack was superior to defence. In 1906, the Kaiser, Franz Josef I, appointed Conrad von Hötzendorf as Chief of Staff.

The post was challenging. Managing the multinational army required significant co-ordination skills and political intelligence, and up to the outbreak of war Conrad was faced with bringing the Austro-Hungarian Army to the peak of its condition. In 1914, he had to accept the fact that the war would be prosecuted on several fronts bordering the old empire. Conrad advocated an aggressive stance against Serbia, as well as the old rivals, Italy.

In war, Conrad von Hötzendorf commanded the Imperial and Royal (*Kaiserlich und Könglich* or k.u.k.) forces, and had a free hand in its prosecution. Respected, his advice was sought in diplomatic relations, though these were sometimes strained with their German allies. The tension was particularly evident in discussions involving the course of the war as demanded by General Falkenhayn, and at times relationships between the two commanders became very strained.

DID YOU KNOW?

Von Hötzendorf became part of the imperial circle when he came to the attention of Archduke Franz Ferdinand, especially as both shared the view that the Austro-Hungarian Army was desperately in need of modernisation.

As a military commander, von Hötzendorf fought the Serbian Army almost to extinction in 1914–15 and faced the Russians in Galicia. Then, with the entry of Italy into the war, he was challenged by a difficult supply chain and topography of an Alpine campaign. The campaign in Galicia was particularly tricky, when in 1914, attacking in the northern part of the sector, the Russian General Ivanov's forces punctured his lines to the south, pushing the Imperial and Royal forces back to the Carpathians, and losing the fortress of Przemyśl. This ground would be hard fought over; regained in 1915 in the Gorlice–Tarnów Offensive with significant German participation, it was once more lost in the successes of the Brusilov Offensive in June 1916. Nevertheless, von Hötzendorf was elevated to field marshal in 1916.

He was relieved on 1 March 1917 by the new Kaiser, Karl I, who had succeeded Franz Josef on his death on 21 November 1916. Von Hötzendorf's views on the conduct of the war were at odds with the new Kaiser's, who associated the old general with the outbreak of the conflict. The field marshal was redeployed as army group commander in the Tyrol, but a planned attack against the Italians in June 1918 was a failure. He was recalled from the front in July.

OTTOMAN EMPIRE

THE OTTOMAN EMPIRE was courted by both sides in the run up to war, but, largely due to diplomatic failures by the Entente, was bound to the Central Powers in 1914.

OVERVIEW OF THE OTTOMAN ARMY

The Ottoman Empire had existed since the thirteenth century, but was contracting fast. When finally committed to the Central Powers, the Ottomans' position was originally defensive, on three fronts: in the Caucasus against the Russians; in the Middle East from Palestine to Mesopotamia against the British and empire troops and Arab militias; and in the Dardanelles against the French and British.

The Ottoman forces were mobilised in August 1914 with initially three armies, growing to five in 1915. The soldiers in these armies were multinational, hardy but ill-equipped and doughty fighters. In 1914, the First and Second Armies served in Thrace to the west of Constantinople, facing the enemies of the Balkan Wars, and in 1915, they defended both shores of the Dardanelles and Bosphorus (the Second Army later serving in the Caucasus). The Third Army served in north-east Anatolia throughout its existence, while the Fourth Army, formed in September 1914, was sent to Syria and took part in the expedition against the British in the Suez Canal zone in late 1914. The Fifth Army, established on 25 March 1915, formed the main defence of the Dardanelles against the Allied attacks. Three other armies, the Sixth, Seventh (both formed in 1915) and Eighth (formed in 1917), saw service in Mesopotamia (Iraq), Palestine and Syria.

THE COMMANDERS

Mustafa Kemal Pasha

Mustafa Kemal was one of the Young Turks, a group committed to change within the Ottoman Empire in 1907. Kemal served in the Ottoman Army through several years of war: he fought in the Italo-Turkish War of 1911–12 that saw the Ottoman possessions in Africa shrink further. He also had an active command role in the Balkan Wars of 1912–13.

By March 1914, Kemal had risen to the rank of lieutenant colonel and was appointed to the command of the 19th Division, part of the Fifth Army. Kemal was an inspirational leader and on at least two occasions he led his men from the front in repelling the Allies.

I WAS THERE

Of the forces which the enemy brought in his ships only a remnant are left. I presume he intends to bring others. Therefore we must drive those now in front of us into the sea.

Mustafa Kemal Pasha, orders to the 57th Infantry Regiment, Gallipoli, 27 April 1915[20]

Though his role in the Gallipoli campaign has been reassessed by historians, he still emerges as a powerful force in the defence of the heights of Sari Bair in particular, where he successfully limited the Allied attacks in April and August 1915. Indeed, it was in Gallipoli that Kemal built his reputation. After Gallipoli, Kemal served in the Caucasus, commanding the XVI Corps of the Ottoman Second Army, which was severely under pressure by the Russians. Kemal launched his own successful counter-offensive in August 1916, and rose to command first the Second Army and then the Seventh Army in Palestine a year later, facing Allenby's offensives as part of Erich von Falkenhayn's Yildirim army group. Kemal resigned his command when his report on the graveness of the Palestine front was ignored in Constantinople. In 1917 he travelled with Crown Prince Mehmed Vahideddin to Germany; later, the now Sultan Mehmed VI gave him command of the Seventh Army in Palestine, in August 1918. As Kemal Atatürk, he was later to lead post-Imperial Turkey.

I WAS THERE

Those heroes that shed their blood and lost their lives ... You are now lying in the soil of a friendly country. Therefore rest in peace.

Kemal Atatürk (formerly Mustafa Kemal Pasha), speaking at Gallipoli, 1934[21]

NOTES

1   Aitken, Max, *Politicians and the War*, Vol. I (London, 1928).

2   Churchill, Winston S., *The World Crisis 1911–1918* (London, 1931), p. 140.

3   French, Field Marshal Sir John, *1914* (London, 1919).

4   'Ninth Despatch of Field Marshal Sir John French', *London Gazette*, 1 November 1915.

5   'Second Despatch of Field Marshal Sir Douglas Haig', *London Gazette Supplement*, 29 December 1916.

6   Haig, Field Marshal Sir Douglas, *Special Order of the Day. To All Ranks of the British Army in France and Flanders*, General Headquarters, 11 April 1918.

7   Allenby, Sir Edmund, 'The Fall of Jerusalem', in Horne, Charles F. (ed.), *Source Records of the Great War*, Vol. V (New York, 1923).

8   Jackson, John Hampden, *Clemenceau and the Third Republic* (London, 1948).

9   Joffre, General Joseph, 'First Battle of the Marne, Special Order of the Day', in Horne, Charles F. (ed.), *Source Records of the Great War*, Vol. II (New York, 1923).

10 Liddell-Hart, B.H., *Reputations* (London, 1928).

11 Nicholas II, Abdication Statement, 15 March 1917, reported in *The Times*, 19 March 1917.

12 Alexei Brusilov, in Horne, Charles F. (ed.), *Source Records of the Great War*, Vol. IV (New York, 1923).

13 General Armando Diaz, *Bollettino della Vittoria* (Final Address of the Chief of the Army Staff), 4 November 1918.

14 President Woodrow Wilson, 'Fourteen Points', speech to a joint session of the United States Congress, 8 January 1918.

15 Vandiver, Frank E., *Black Jack: The Life and Times of John J. Pershing*, Vol. II (Texas, 1977), p. 724.

16 Wilhelm II, *The Kaiser's Memoirs* (New York & London, 1922), p. 250.

17 Walder, David, *The Chanak Affair* (London, 1969), p. 21.

18 Jessen, Olaf, *Die Moltkes: Biographie einer Familie* (Munchen, 2010).

19 Ludendorff, General, *My War Memories 1914–1918*, Vol. II (London, 1919), p. 679.

20 Aspinall-Oglander, Brigadier-General C.F., *Military Operations Gallipoli*, Vol. I, Official History of the War (London, 1929), p. 296.

21 Text of speech given in 1934, memorialised at the battlefield of Gallipoli, Turkey.

SELECT BIBLIOGRAPHY

Armstrong, H.C., *Grey Wolf* (London, 1932)

Bourne, J.M., *Who's Who in World War One* (London, 2002)

Brusilov, A.A., *A Soldier's Notebook, 1914–1918* (London, 1930)

Churchill, Sir Winston S., *Great Contemporaries* (London, 1937)

Dupuy, T.N., *The Military Lives of Hindenburg and Ludendorff of Imperial Germany* (New York, 1970)

Falkenhayn, General Erich von, *General Headquarters 1914–16 and its Critical Decisions* (London, 1919)

Falls, Cyril, *Marshal Foch* (London, 1939)

Falls, Cyril, *Caporetto 1917* (London, 1966)

Gardner, Brian, *Allenby* (London, 1965)

Griffiths, Richard, *Marshal Pétain* (London, 1994)

Haythornwaite, Phillip J., *The World War One Sourcebook* (London, 1992)

Herwig, H.H. & Heyman, N.M., *Biographical Dictionary of World War I* (Westport, Connecticut, 1982)

Holmes, Richard, *The Little Field Marshal: Sir John French* (London, 1981)

Joffre, Marshal J.J.C., *The Memoirs of Marshal Joffre* (London, 1927)

Keegan, J. & Wheatcroft, A., *Who's Who in Military History* (London, 1976)

Liddell Hart, Sir Basil, *Reputations* (London, 1928)

Liddell Hart, Sir Basil, *Foch: Man of Orleans* (London, 1931)

Lottman, H.R., *Pétain: Hero or Traitor, the Untold Story* (New York, 1985)

Ludendorff, General E., *My War Memories* (London, 1919)

Pershing, General J.J., *My Experience in the World War* (London, 1931)

Sheffield, Gary, *The Chief, Douglas Haig and the British Army* (London, 2011)

Terrain, John, *Douglas Haig: The Educated Soldier* (London, 1963)

Wavell, Field Marshal Viscount, *Allenby, Soldier & Stateman* (London, 1946)

www.firstworldwar.com

Discover more books in this series ...

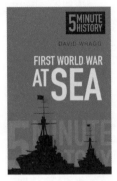

978-0-7509-5567-6   £5.00

978-0-7509-5571-3   £5.00

978-0-7524-9322-0   £5.00

978-0-7524-9321-3   £5.00

Visit our website and discover thousands
of other History Press books.

www.thehistorypress.co.uk